Broom Casting For Creative Jewelry And Metal Work

Bradford M. Smith

Broom Casting

For Creative Jewelry and Metal Work

Discover the rush of pouring melted silver into a wet broom
to produce intriguing fun, icicle-like shapes that add
a fresh creativity to jewelry designs

First soft cover edition printed 2015

The material in this volume should be used only as a learning guide. No element of these procedures is intended to negate the need for proper clothing, dust masks, and eye protection. All generally accepted industry safety procedures should be followed when using torches and tools or doing casting in the jewelry shop.

The Author and Publisher disclaim any liability for injury or unexpected results that might occur while attempting to follow suggestions in this publication.

ISBN-10: 0988285835

ISBN-13: 978-0-9882858-3-5

DEDICATION

For whatever artistic abilities I have in jewelry and photography, I wish to give thanks to my Mom. For my underlying belief that a person can accomplish anything they really want to do, I am grateful to my Dad.

This project would not have been possible without the constant support, the unquestioned love, and the active collaboration from my wife and daughters.

The skills I've developed in creating jewelry are based on the expertise of my mentor, Anthony Chavez. I thank him for urging me to become a teacher and sharing the fun of making jewelry with others.

My "masters level" training, as I think of it, came from eagerly reading the "Orchid Digest" every day for about six years. "Orchid Digest" is a fabulous repository of jewelry making knowledge distributed by way of a discussion list curated by Dr. Hanuman Aspler. "Orchid Digest" also maintains an archive of over 250,000 articles on jewelry skills and techniques.

I'd like to thank the late Stuart Chalfant from the Conejo Gem and Mineral Club in Thousand Oaks, California for his presentation that first introduced me to this delightful way of burning brooms. It was a long time ago, but I can still remember him with a big white chef's hat in the front of the room cracking jokes while pouring hot metal.

Finally, I want to express my gratitude to all of the wonderful students who have taken my classes. Teaching others has become a rewarding and fulfilling part of my life. I especially want to thank those students who have allowed me to show their broom cast creations in this volume.

ALSO BY THE AUTHOR

BENCH TIPS FOR JEWELRY MAKING

ACCESSORIES FOR THE FOREDOM AND DREMEL

MAKING DESIGN STAMPS FOR JEWELRY

BENCH TIPS FOR JEWELRY MAKING

THE RELUCTANT FARMER OF WHIMSEY HILL

http:// amazon.com/author/bradfordsmith

CONTENTS

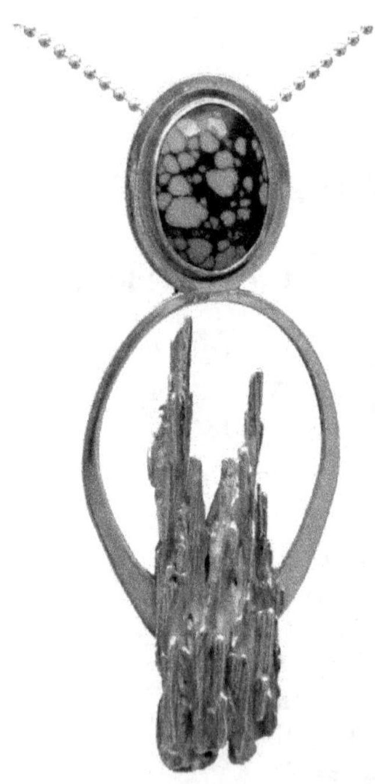

Turquoise Pendant by Bradford Smith
that incorporates a broom casting
Lapidary Journal Jewelry Artist Magazine
Step-By-Step Broom Casting – June 2007

PREFACE

As a studio jeweler and a classroom instructor, I typically work with detailed directions, exacting ratios, precise layout lines, and delicate gemstone settings. But sometimes I feel it liberating to just play with the metal, such as melting a few ounces and pouring it randomly into a broom.

Discover the rush of pouring molten silver to get marvelous icicle-like shapes to make great pendants and earrings. Yes, this is broom casting. Learn the basics of melting metal, protecting it from oxidation, modifying the irregular shapes for your jewelry designs, and cleaning & polishing your piece to a bright finish. These are the same techniques used for making alloy ingots, cuttlebone casting, sand casting, and lost wax casting.

The material in the chapters that follow should be used only as a learning guide. Nothing in these instructions is intended to negate the need for proper clothing, ventilation, safety equipment, and eye protection. All generally accepted industry safety procedures should be followed when melting and pouring metal in the jewelry shop.

Happy hammering!

- Brad

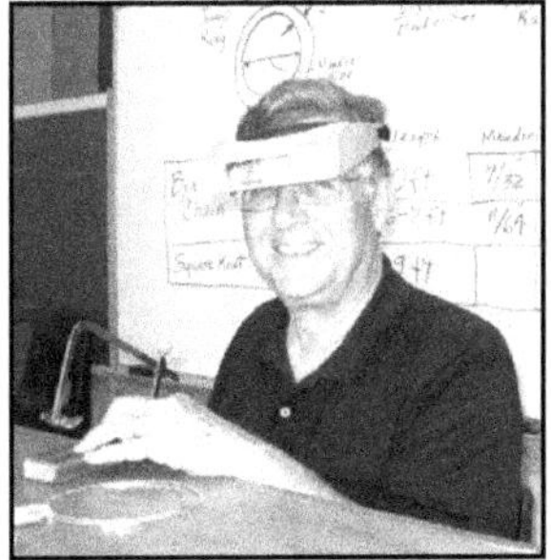

WARNING

Metal Working Tools and Procedures Are Dangerous

Do not attempt procedures described in this book without professional supervision.

All local and industry safety procedures should be followed.

CHAPTER 1

INTRODUCTION

Content

Broom casting is one of the most popular topics I have taught over the years. Students love the process – for who doesn't get a thrill out of pouring silver into a broom. The popularity is also due to the wonderfully unusual pieces that result from the process.

But I have noticed that many people who have tried the technique are a little reluctant to try broom casting by themselves. Perhaps they don't feel familiar enough with the process steps and the equipment. My purpose in the following chapters is to fully explain the process, to show proper use of all the equipment, to offer tips for fabricating jewelry from the castings, and to share examples of finished jewelry made from them.

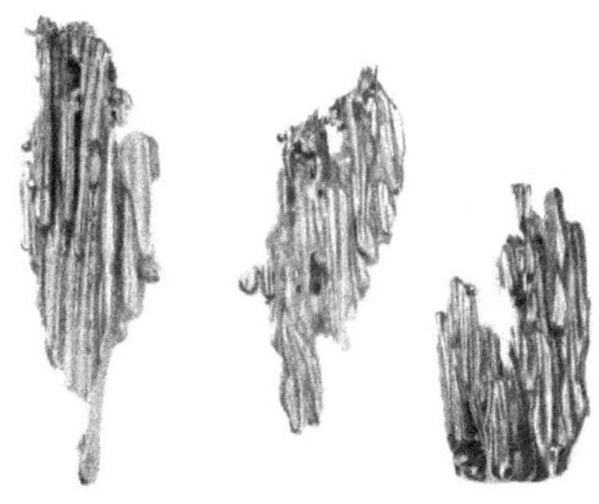

Casting in a Broom

Making jewelry involves a multitude of skills, many of which require considerable time and practice to master. Becoming accomplished at soldering, setting faceted stones, producing vibrant enamels, engraving your initials, lost wax casting, and cutting your own gemstones are just a few of the many skills that require careful study, serious practice, and attention to detail.

But there are a few other jewelry making skills that are quite the opposite. They are relatively easy to learn, produce quick results, stimulate the imagination, and are just plain fun to do. Everyone has their own examples. My three favorites are fold forming, roll patterning, and broom casting.

Techniques like these can be learned well enough in an hour or two to be able to produce usable pieces with intriguing geometries and textures that beg to be designed into finished jewelry. Each piece is a creative accident. They spark the imagination and challenge your creative mind. Sometimes very little extra work is needed to make finished jewelry. Solder on a few findings, add a gemstone or two, fashion a bail, and you have created a piece of jewelry that is unique, fresh, and elegant.

Few techniques are more straightforward than broom casting. Only basic equipment that is available in most jewelry shops is needed. Simply melt an ounce or two of scrap silver and pour it into a wet broom. The result is marvelous icicle-like shapes that make great pendants and earrings.

Broom cast pieces have the added dimension that they are born of fire. And for those who have not done it before, it is really quite a rush to pour your first melting dish of molten silver.

Safety

A note of caution is in order as you begin to do any broom casting. Working with molten metal carries a significant safety risk. The metal is at about 1800 degrees, so any spill can be dangerous. Contact with the hot tools is an ever-present hazard.

A familiarity with large torches is useful. The quantity of hot metal involved increases the level of danger from fire or accident. I would suggest you not attempt to do your first broom casting alone. And it is important to have all of the proper safety equipment on hand.

Safety starts with your personal protection. Wear safety goggles, a heavy apron, and closed-toed shoes. Assume that everything in the work area is hot. Test for heat before trying to pick up anything with bare hands.

Your safety also depends upon keeping focused on the task at hand. Don't rush. Control any distractions. Ask people not to talk or ask questions until the job is finished.

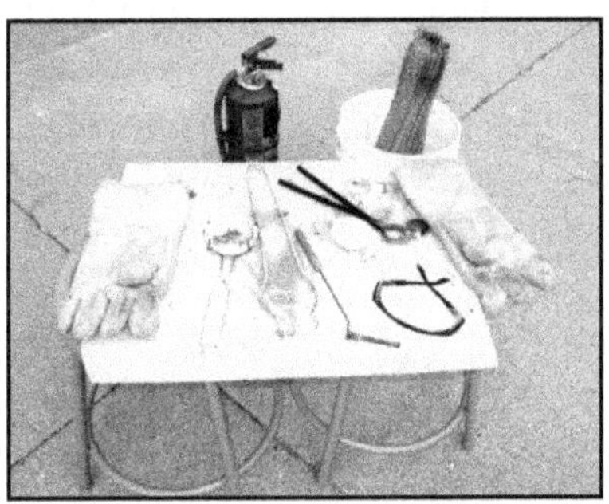

Examples of safety equipment to have available are:

Fire extinguisher	Tongs
Heat resistant gloves	Closed-toed shoes
Safety goggles	Heavy apron

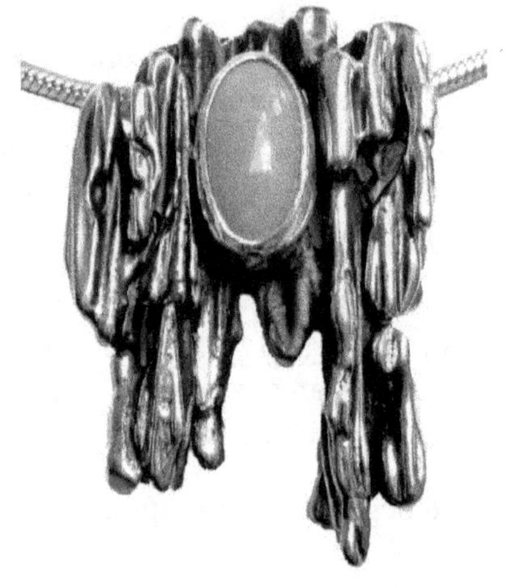

Pendant by Bradford Smith
Sterling silver with turquoise stone

CHAPTER 2

HOW IT'S DONE

Assemble Casting Equipment

Tools and supplies you will need to do the casting include:

Metal for casting	Utility pliers
Melting dish or crucible	Cutters
Carbon rod for stirring	Borax flux
Torch with a large tip	Tongs
Copper or steel binding wire	Water
Two clean five-gallon buckets	Coffee cup
Broom holder	Fire brick

A natural bristle (straw) floor broom. No plastic bristles!

Prepare A Melting Dish

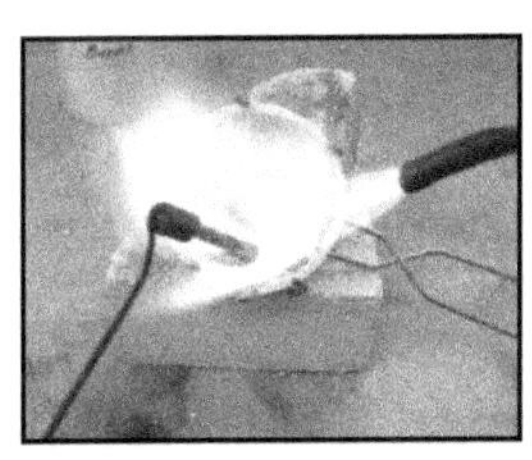

A new melting dish or crucible must be given a protective coat of borax before its first use. The coating extends the life of the ceramic surface of your crucible or melting dish. Once it has been coated, it generally never has to be redone.
A step-by-step procedure for this is given in Chapter 5.

Prepare The Broom

Select a large natural bristle straw or cornstalk floor broom. Plastic brooms will not work. The bristles will melt. Saw off most of the broom handle, leaving a stub about 3" long. Cut all stitching and pull the strings from the broom. This allows you to gather the bristles of the flat broom together and bind them with a length of small gauge wire into a round bundle.

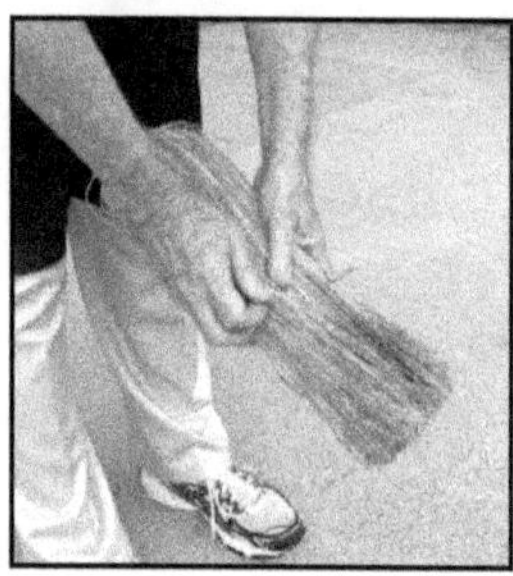

Position the wire about six inches down from the top of the bristles and compress the bristles into a cylindrical shape about 3" to 4" in diameter. Too tight a bind may not allow the molten metal to penetrate the bristles very easily, whereas too loose a bind may allow the molten metal to flow all the way through the broom.

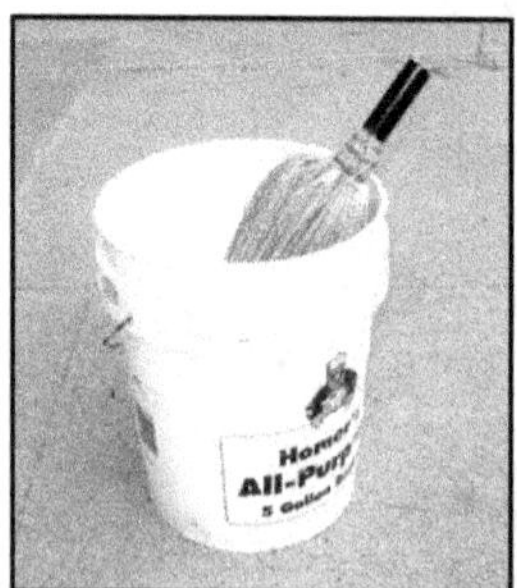

Finally, fill a 5-gallon plastic bucket about two-thirds full of water and soak the broom for about 30 to 40 minutes before casting. This helps to keep the bristles from bursting into flame as the hot metal hits them, allowing you to get five to eight pours out of each broom.

Supporting The Broom

A reliable way is needed to hold the broom steady and in an upright position so that the molten metal can be easily poured into the bristles. There are a number of ways to do this. Two that I have used are shown below. If you start to do a lot of broom casting, you may be interested in the holder described in Chapter 5.

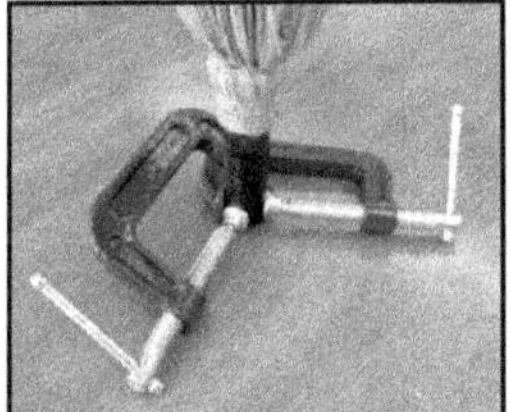

One easy way to support the broom is to use two 3-inch C-clamps at right angles. The only thing to keep in mind when selecting the clamps is that they need to fit into the catch pan or bucket that you will be using.

A second approach is to fill a metal can with clean one-inch pebbles and push the broomstick into it. This can is about seven inches in diameter. Use large pebbles, not sand or small stones. Small granules will become mixed with any spilled metal and make it very difficult to re-use the metal for additional castings.

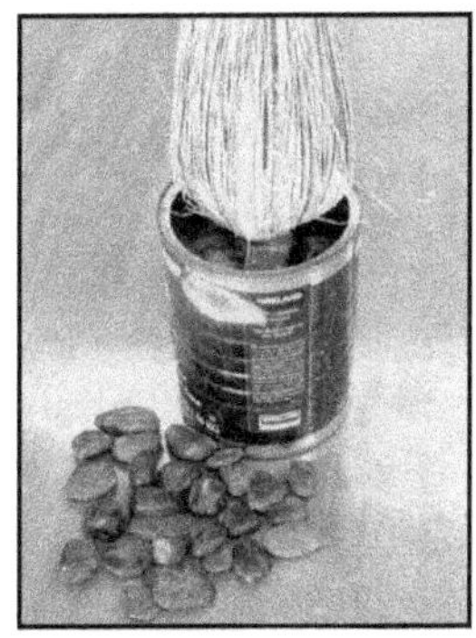

Containing Any Spills

When metal is poured into the top of a broom, the process is rarely perfect and spills of molten metal will often happen. Droplets can roll off the top of the broom, or some of the pour can dribble through the bristles to come out lower down on the side. Some arrangement is necessary to catch spills safely, make it easy to recover small pieces of precious metal, and allow for the metal to cool without risk of fire.

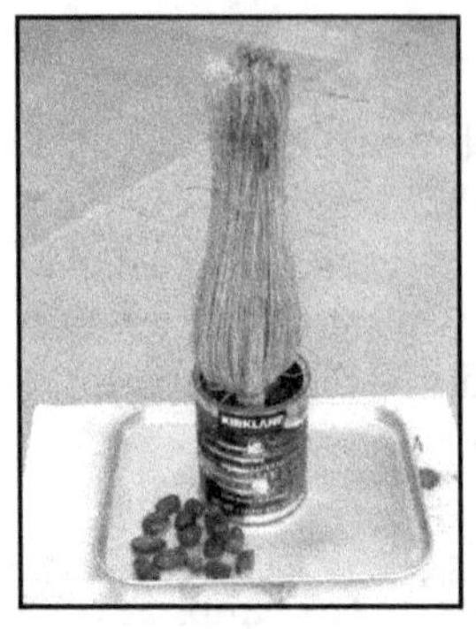

There are two easy solutions. The first is to do your pouring within a large metal tray. Anything with a lip around the edge and dimensions larger than fifteen inches should work well – for instance, a large baking pan.

Metal trays should be placed on a heat resistant surface. Molten metal falling into an empty metal pan on a wooden bench will burn the bench (I've done that). My preference is to have an inch or two of water in the tray so spills are immediately caught and cooled to a safe handling temperature. If using water, look for a pan with large sidewalls, like a jelly roll pan.

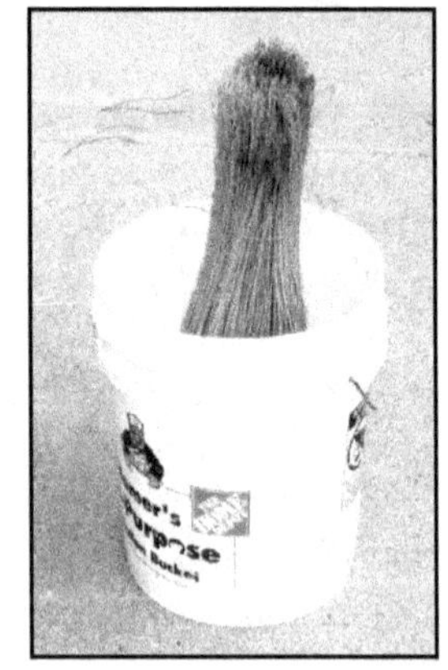

A second method for catching spills is to use a five-gallon plastic bucket. This is my favorite because they are more readily available than large trays. But with plastic, it's best to have four to six inches of water in the bucket to prevent a large glob of metal from melting through the bottom.

Set Up For Casting

As mentioned earlier, any metal casting can be hazardous and should not be attempted by a novice. It's best to ask a friend with casting experience to give you a hand the first couple times. You should have the proper equipment and be familiar with torches, with melting, and with pouring hot metal.

Broom casting is best done outside as it can be a messy process which produces a fair amount of smoke.

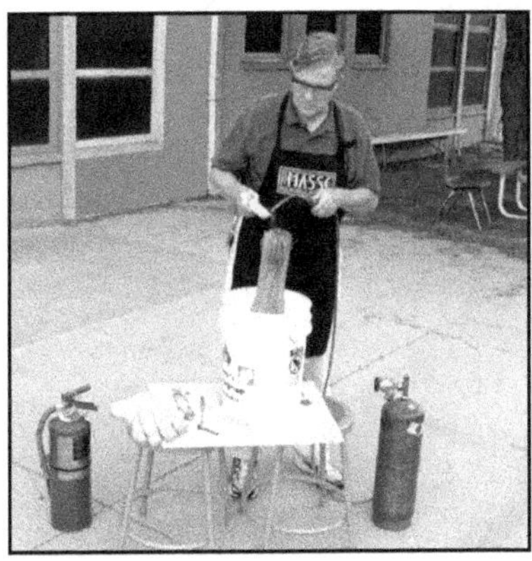

Heating The Metal

Heat two or three ounces of metal in the crucible. The tip of the flame's blue cone is the hottest part of the flame and should be held about a quarter inch over the metal. Be careful to keep the flame on the melt at all times.

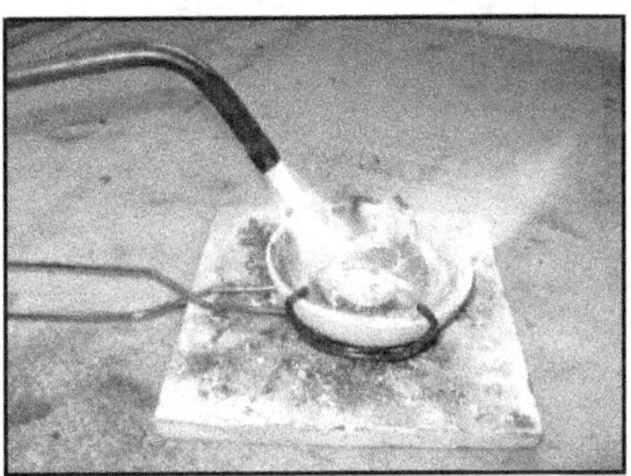

When the metal starts to melt, add a pinch of borax flux. As the metal melts into a liquid and balls up, stir with a carbon rod to mix and to test for lumps of unmelted metal in the bottom of the crucible. Continue to heat until thoroughly melted.

The proper pouring temperature is reached when the melt rolls around freely in the crucible and the flux appears to be swirling around on top of the melt.

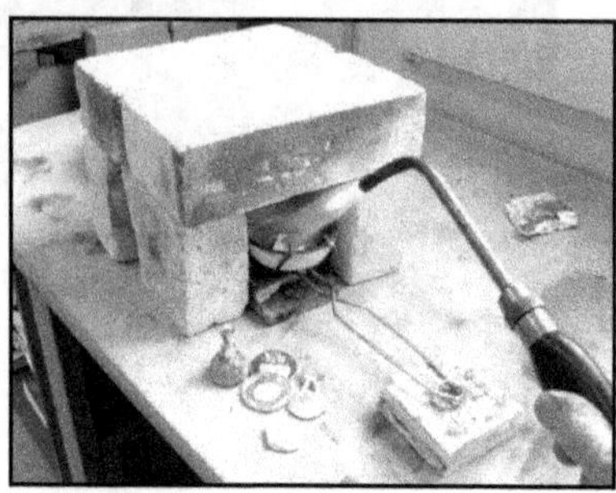

If there is a breeze while you are heating the metal, a small oven can be made from fire bricks to help reflect heat back into the melting dish.

Making The Pour

It's important to keep the flame on the melting dish all the time while pouring. Pour a slow steady stream of metal into the bristles while moving the crucible in a slow circular motion over the bristles. Practice is required when pouring into the broom. If all the metal is poured into one place, it will produce a large cluster of casting pieces, and if the movement across the broom is too fast, the result will be numerous small casting pieces.

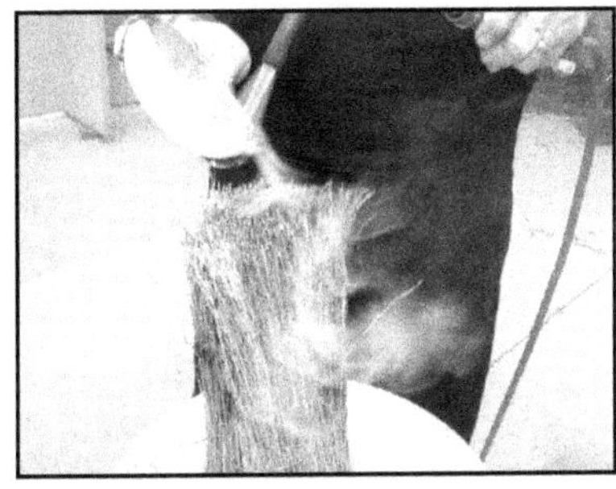

When finished pouring, set the hot melting dish onto a firebrick to cool. Then douse the smoking broom with several cups of water from the bucket.

Recovering The Castings

After the metal has cooled, unbind the bristles, and retrieve as many casting pieces as you can find. Use caution because some pieces may still be hot. This should be done over a clean heat-resistant surface that makes it easy to recover all of the precious metal pieces however small they may be.

A concrete slab or a large, flat baking tray will work, but my preference is to use a five-gallon plastic bucket with a few inches of water in the bottom. Unbind the broom, lower it into the bucket, and shake to dislodge the castings. Any remaining pieces can be found by carefully picking through the bristles.

Select the cast pieces you wish to keep, rebind the broom, and cast again. All of the undesirable pieces can be re-melted with enough new metal to make a full pour.

Each broom will generally give you five or more castings. If the top of the broom burns away irregularly in a few places, a quick trim with heavy shears will renew the top surface.

When you have completely finished the casting session for the day, it's worthwhile to go through the bristles of the broom again to retrieve any small bits of overlooked metal. Finally, set the broom outside to dry for your next casting session.

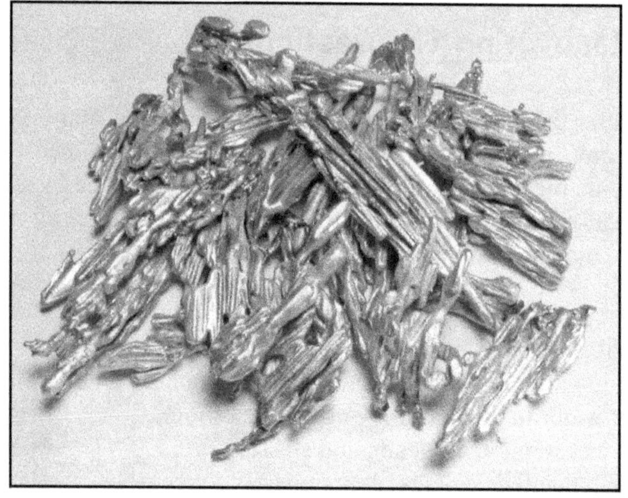

Results of a good casting session

CHAPTER 3

CLEANING UP THE CASTINGS

The broom cast pieces will need a little clean-up before you will be able to select those to use for jewelry making. Some pieces will have charred broom bristles still embedded in the metal. Others may be discolored. Most will have a dull satin finish. Here is how to quickly clean-up the castings.

I start by picking out all the fragments of broom bristles. If they are numerous, I use a water bath to float them off. Next I use a needle, stylus, or set of fine tweezers remove all bristles that are embedded in the metal. A brief soak in the pickle pot will then take off most of the dark discoloration. Neutralize the acid with a dip into baking soda and water.

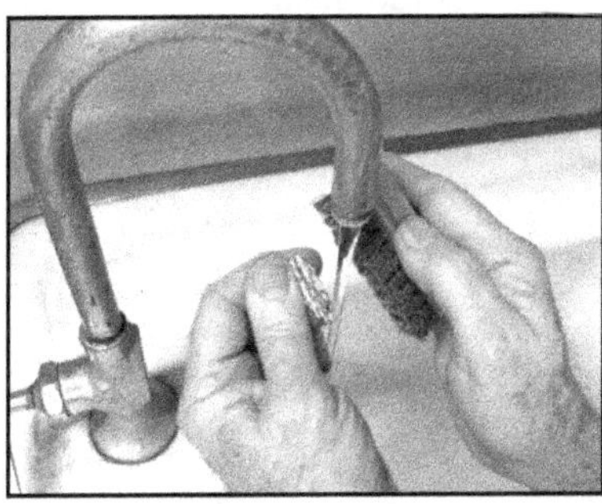

A quick way to shine up the surface of these irregular broom cast pieces is to scrub them with a fine brass brush and water. Do not try this with a dry brush, as it will leave a brassy color on the silver pieces that is hard to remove.

Rough Shaping

With the castings clean and bright, it is easy to see the details of each piece. Evaluate each to pick out the better shapes to be used for making jewelry. Closely study the ones that are selected to be sure all appendages are solidly joined to the main body to provide the strength needed to be used in your jewelry design.

Look for appendages that are not needed. These can be removed quickly with wire cutters or a jewelers saw. Smaller blobs can be filed smooth or sanded off with a Dremel motor tool or Foredom flexshaft.

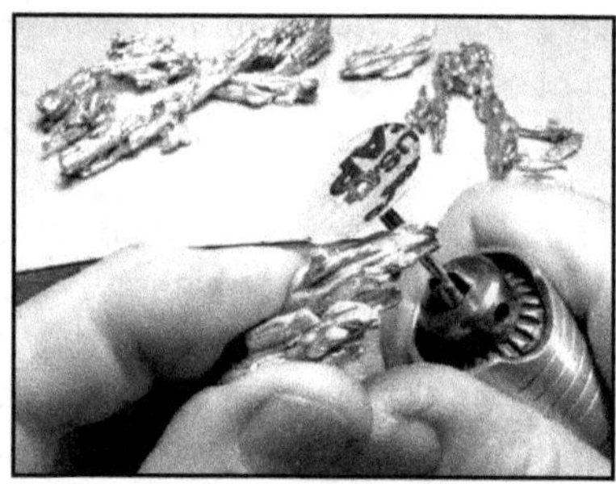

Lastly, smooth any scratches left from sanding. Small silicone polishing wheels make this an easy job. They come in several different abrasive levels and in different shapes (coin, knife, cylinder, point, etc) to match the geometry of the area being polished. Your pieces are now ready to be incorporated into new jewelry designs.

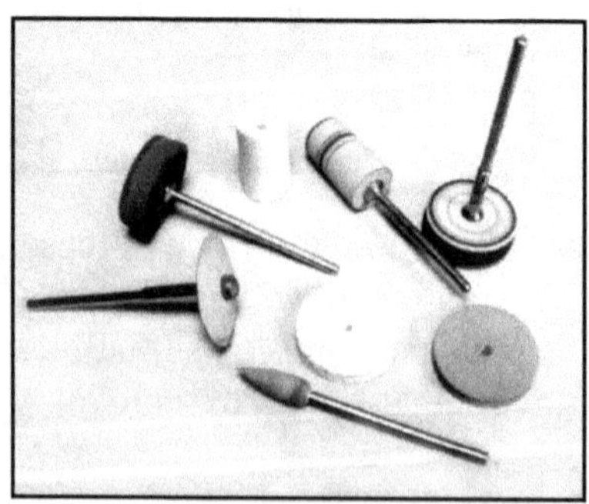

CHAPTER 4

MODIFYING CASTING SHAPES

Previous chapters have discussed about how the curiously random shapes generated by broom casting can spark creativity. Examining the results of a pour is always a pleasure. Ideas for new jewelry form quickly.

However, there will be problems as well. Large masses can be difficult to subdivide, mounting gemstones on an irregular shape is challenging, some pieces may have voids or lack balance, and finding duplicate shapes for earrings can be difficult. Here are a few ways to deal with these problems.

Subdividing

Some pieces might initially seem unusable because of their large size. Before remelting them, give a second look to see if they can be cut into smaller, more useful pieces.

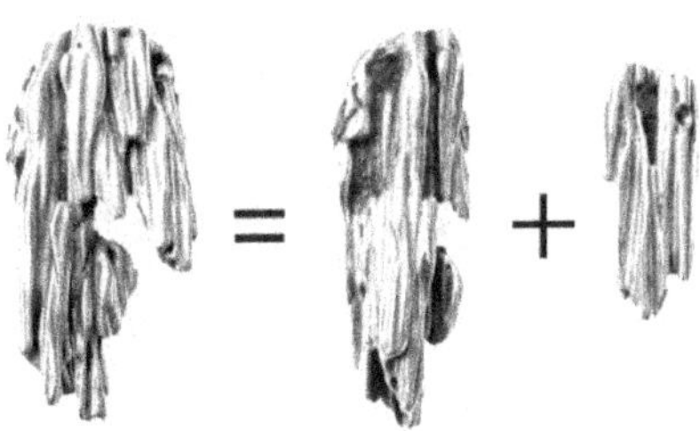

Now it's easy to think, "I'll just saw it in two," but this is not always easy. A broom casting can frequently be 6 - 8mm thick and will require quite a bit of effort to cut in half. Also, many broom cast shapes are hard to hold, so any movement of the piece will result in a broken blade.

I use a coarse blade for thick sections, perhaps a #2. And it's always best to provide lubrication to keep the blade cool and the teeth sharp. Wax or a cut lube will work, but cutting thicker metal calls for more of a machine shop approach. My choice for lubrication when cutting a heavy section is motor oil or the handy 3-in-1 utility oil.

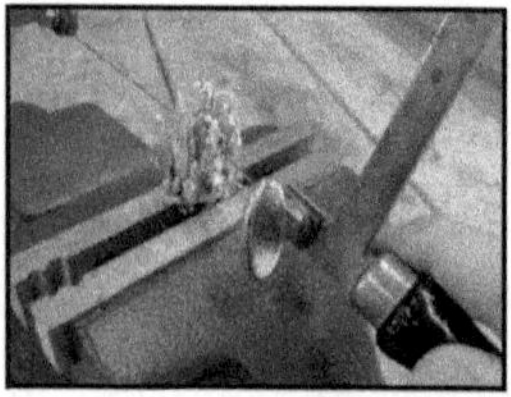

If attempting either type of cut, it's worth clamping the unwanted segment of the casting in a bench vise if possible. This holds the piece rigidly and frees both hands for sawing.

Mounting Gemstones

In some instances, you will want to remove a section of the casting to make room for a gemstone. However, if a saw blade or a file cannot be used, your alternatives disappear rapidly. Don't underestimate the time and trouble of doing this.

Cutting out excess metal with a bur is laborious and risks damaging adjacent areas if the tool is not held firmly or if it happens to catch an edge and run. Here, I use a wheel bur.

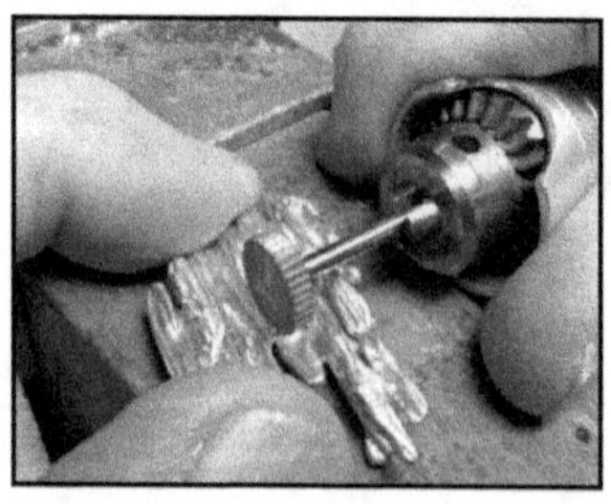

Removing excess metal from the interior of a piece with a bur is possible, but it is also a challenge. When a small area must be carved out, I prefer to first use a round ball bur for more control. Then to cut a flat bottom, you will need a bur that cuts on the end as well as the side. One of my favorites is an inverse cone bur. Here, I use one that is 3mm in diameter.

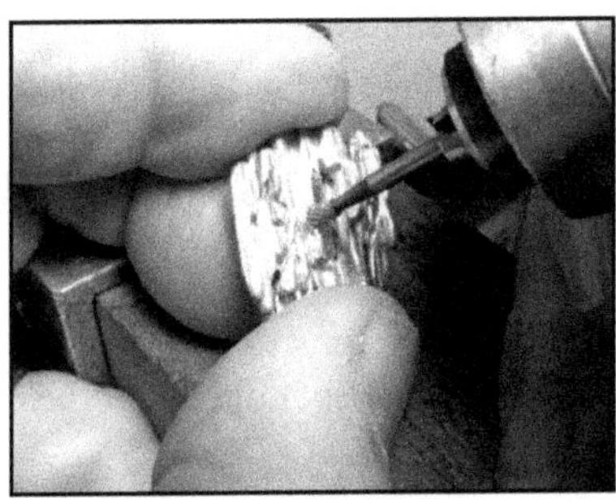

Modifying Shapes

Often an otherwise beautiful shape is marred by a minor void or is a little off balance. This can easily be corrected by finding one or more small broom cast extras that can be soldered on to fill the void or add more bulk where needed.

Here, three separate pieces are combined to produce the desired shape. Hard solder should be used to avoid any difficulty with subsequent soldering of prong settings, bezels, or other findings.

Producing Duplicates

Because the broom casting technique is completely random and produces one-of-a-kind pieces, it is not possible to duplicate a particularly nice shape by simply pouring more metal. This means that it will be quite difficult to produce a pair of earrings let alone a dozen identical dangles for a necklace. But it also means that if you are selling your jewelry, a popular design will be all the more difficult to produce in quantity.

Duplicates of broom cast items can be made if the shape is fairly simple. The first step is to make a rubber mold. Molten wax is then injected into the mold to produce as many copies as are needed.

The lost-wax casting technique is used to cast the waxes in whatever metal is desired. This can be done in some well-equipped jewelry shops but is usually left to a commercial caster. Casters can be found with a Google search or from ads in major jewelry magazines. As I write this, a mold generally costs around $35 and silver castings cost around $2 per gram, which includes metal and labor.

Bear in mind that one limitation of the molding process is that it does not work for all shapes. Molding is limited to the more simple geometric shapes. Molds must be cut so that when the injected wax solidifies, the mold can be opened and the wax removed without breaking the shape. This is not possible for some of the very complicated shapes produced by broom casting.

CHAPTER 5

TIPS FOR EASY CASTING

Stirring Rods

When melting metals for casting, it's important to have something to stir the melt. Stirring ensures a homogeneous mixture. It also lets you check for any lumps of metal that have not yet melted.

A carbon rod is inexpensive solution. It stands up well to high temperatures, will not contaminate the metal, and does not allow silver, bronze, or gold to stick to it. However, there is a major shortcoming. A carbon rod is quite fragile and must be handled gently.

Rods can be purchased from most jewelry supply catalogs and are available from Ebay or Amazon. I prefer the ones that are about the size of a pencil, 0.25 inch (6mm) in diameter.

Other materials can be used to stir the melt but are not as easily available. They include quartz, tungsten, and titanium. Of course in a pinch, you can also use a steel rod, but some of the gold or silver may stick to it, and there is a small possibility that steel may cause some contamination.

Carbon Rod Holder

Carbon rods are my favorite choice for stirring a melt, but they are fragile and break easily. They also get hot. So the main problem with a carbon rod is how to hold it. A pair of pliers will work in a pinch, but if you apply too much pressure, the rod cracks. And if you happen to drop the rod, it usually breaks.

My solution is to make a holder from a piece of 3/16 or 1/8 inch metal wire. Heavy steel clothes hanger wire or a thin brass brazing rod works well. Other alternatives for wire can be found in most local hardware stores.

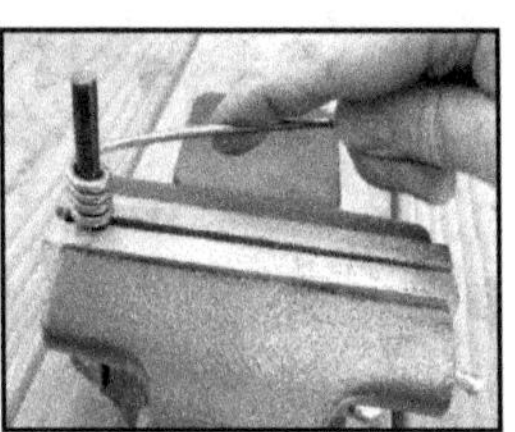

Wind the wire around a mandrel of the right size, like you would wind jump rings. Here I use a 15/64 inch mandrel to fit a 1/4 inch carbon rod. Bend the end of the wire down between the vice jaws to keep the coil from turning on the mandrel as you wind the wire around the mandrel.

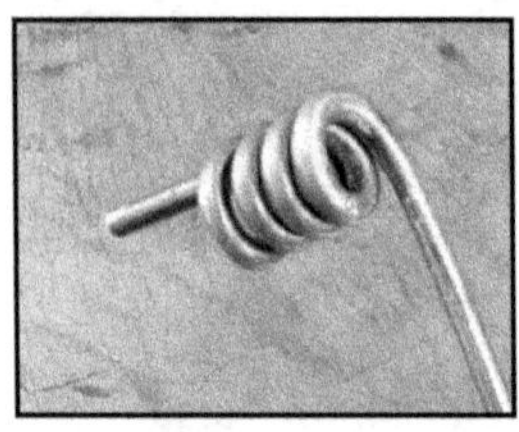

Leave a long tail of wire on the end of the coil to act as a handle. Finish the holder by sticking the tail into a length of wooden dowel or other material to serve as a handle. This makes it easy to use the stirring rod even with bare hands.

Here, a piece of deer antler provides a nice handle.

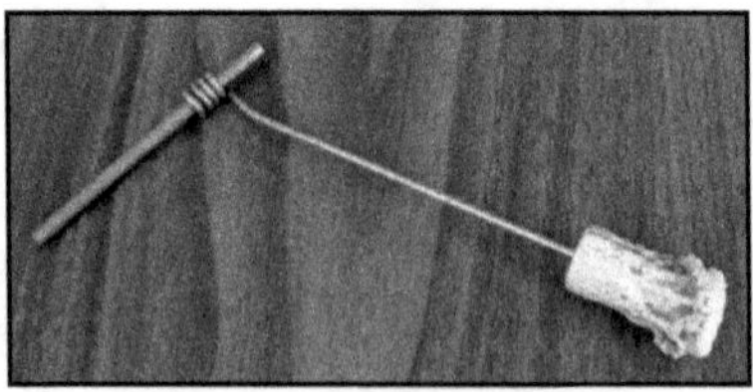

40 Mule Team Borax

While it is easy to order borax from almost any jewelry supply catalog, it is also available locally as a washing powder. 40 Mule Team Borax can still be found in some grocery stores and works well as a flux when melting silver.

Support Stand

If you do a lot of broom casting, you'll appreciate this holder that a friend of mine made for me in welding class. The base is 3/16 inch steel plate with a 5-inch length of steel pipe welded in the center. We trimmed the corners to let it fit into the bottom of a standard five-gallon bucket.

This is a simple welding job using commonly available scrap materials that can be found in most shops. If you know a welder, perhaps you can trade them a piece of jewelry.

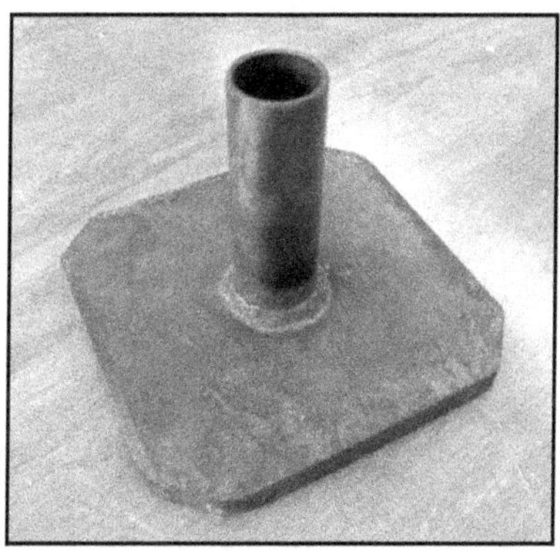

Preparing A Melting Dish

A new melting dish or crucible must be given a protective coating of borax before its first use. Borax extends the life of the ceramic material. Here's how it is done:

The procedure is straightforward. Heat the new melting dish to red with a large torch. Here I'm using an acetylene/air Prest-O-Lite torch with a large #5 nozzle.

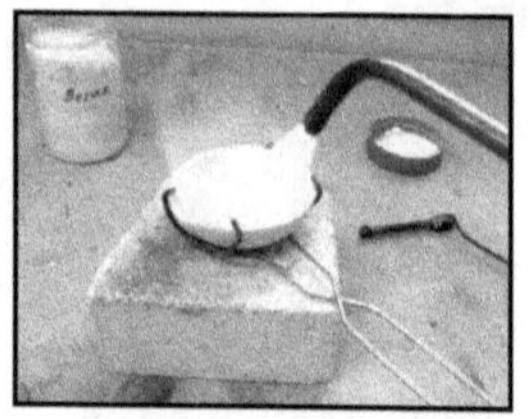

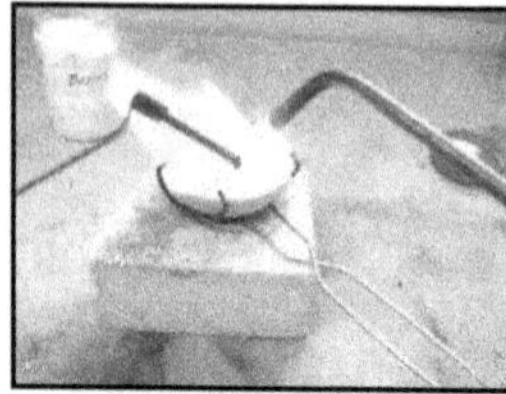

When hot, sprinkle in a half teaspoon of borax, let it melt, and spread it with a carbon rod over all of the interior surface of the dish. Add more borax if needed.

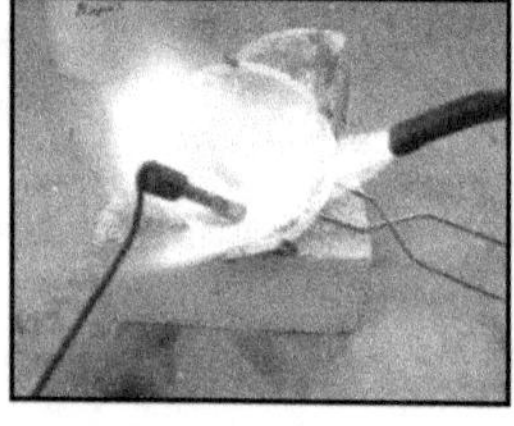

Sometimes you will have to hold the dish at an angle to coat the sides up to the rim. And don't forget to coat the pouring spout itself.

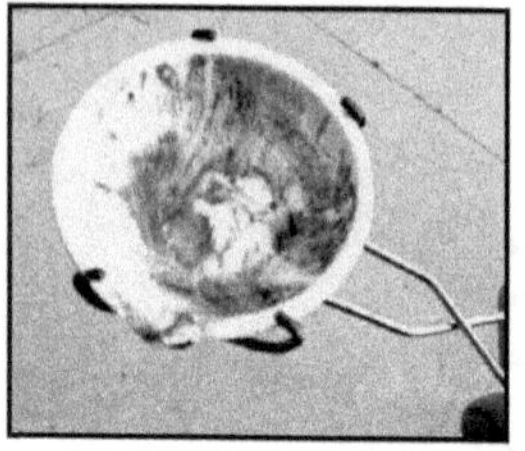

This is the glassy protective coating that is best to have on new crucibles and melting dishes. As the dish is used more and more, the color of the borax coating will change to a dark brick red. This shows that the flux is doing its job – cleaning the copper oxides out of the melt.

Heat-Proof Bench Surface

An inexpensive and very effective heat proof surface for a casting bench can be made using a building material called Hardie Backer Board. It is a fiber reinforced cement sheet that is typically used as a waterproof base for ceramic tiles in bath tubs and shower stalls.

Source For Low Cost Silver

Scrap silver can be used for broom casting. If more metal is needed, there's no reason to buy casting grain with its high fabrication cost. Save some money by buying your silver at a local coin store. They sell bars and rounds in Sterling and .999 pure for just a small amount over the spot price.

I figure I save about $5 per ounce on the fabrication charge, pay no shipping, and support a local business all at the same time. Be sure to specify which metal is preferred - pure silver or Sterling silver. Pure silver will require more heat from the torch.

Melting Dish Types

Melting dishes come in two general types – a dish that is designed to be clamped into a handle with bolt and nut, or a dish that is designed to be used separately to be carried in a spring clamp handle or held with tongs.

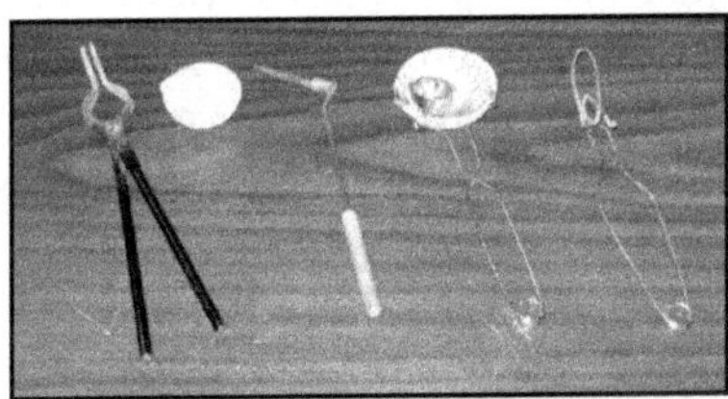

Either works well for broom casting although my preference is to use dishes which are separate from the handle. They are less expensive and allow me to instantly switch dishes in the spring clamp handle to accommodate silver, gold, or bronze without any cross-contamination.

How To Make An Alloy

If you only have pure silver and wish to cast with Sterling, you can easily make the alloy while melting the metal for casting.

Sterling is 92.5 % silver with the remainder usually copper. So all you have to do is add some copper to the melt. The only question is how much?

For every Troy ounce of pure silver, I add 2.5 grams of scrap copper sheet. Then to make the alloy, place the copper on top of the silver in the melting bowl, heat until the metal is fluid, throw in a pinch of borax, and stir well with a carbon rod to ensure a homogeneous mixture. Be sure to keep the flame on the melt until pouring has been completed.

Easy Outside Casting Bench Setup

Some of my broom casting workshops have been given in a general purpose meeting room which does not allow open flames to be used, so our casting is done on a patio just outside the room. The only challenge is how to provide a large heat resistant bench surface for attendees to work on.

My solution is to use one of the conference tables at the facility. To protect the vinyl surface from the heat of the torches, I use sheets of 5/8 inch Hardie Board (see tip on Bench Surface, page 22) that are cut small enough to fit in the trunk of my car.

However, the sheets alone are not sufficient to protect the table's vinyl surface. So I elevate the sheets on blocks of 2x4 scrap wood. This provides ample ventilation between the vinyl and the hot working surface.

CHAPTER 6

EXAMPLE BROOM CASTING JEWELRY

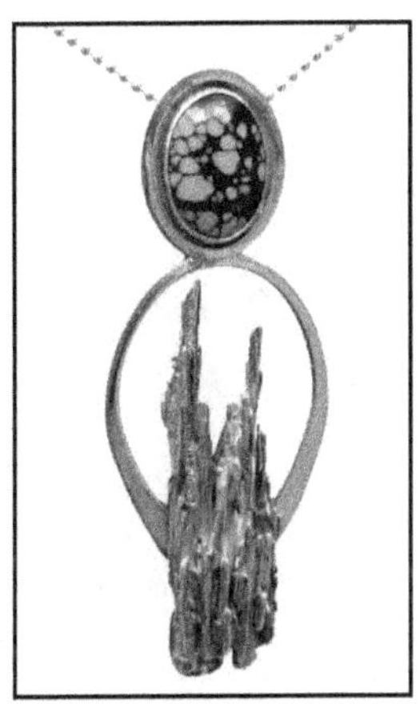

Bradford Smith

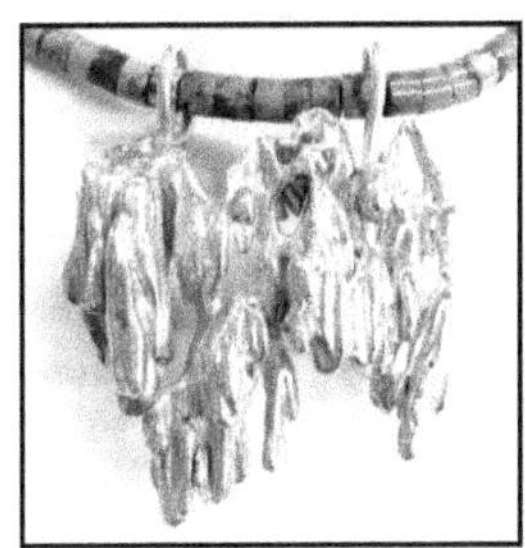

Ana Petrova

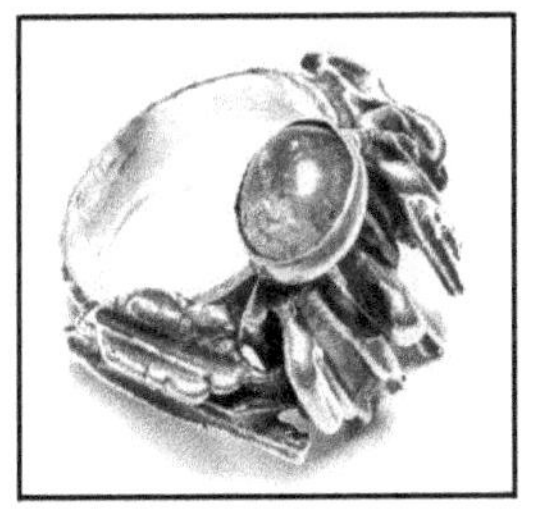

Eva Nathanson

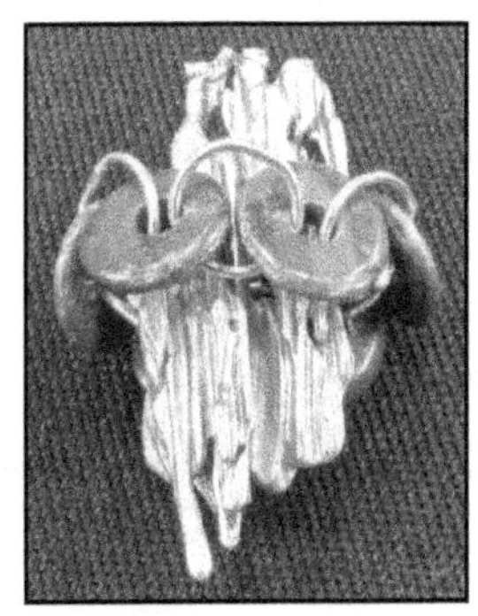

Sara Haium

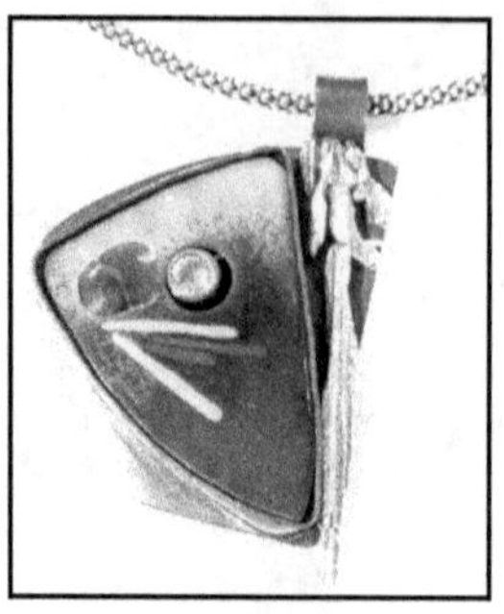

Ana Petrova

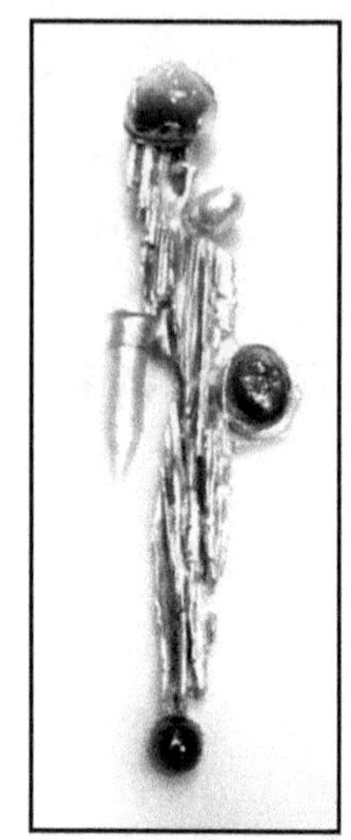

Eva Nathanson

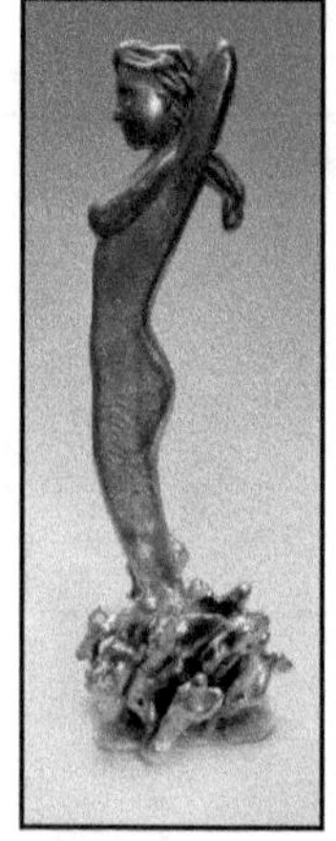

Eva Nathanson

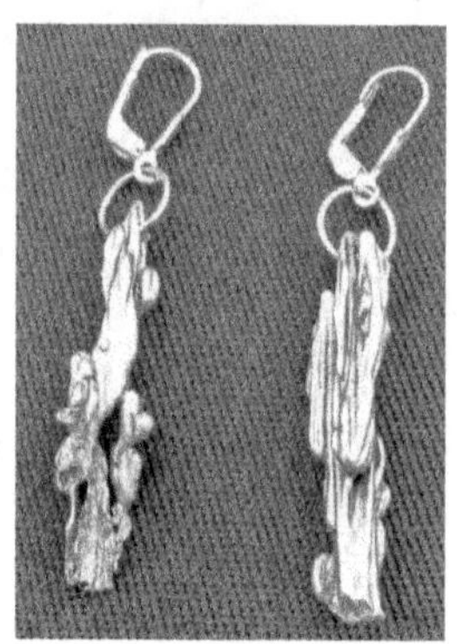

Sara Haium

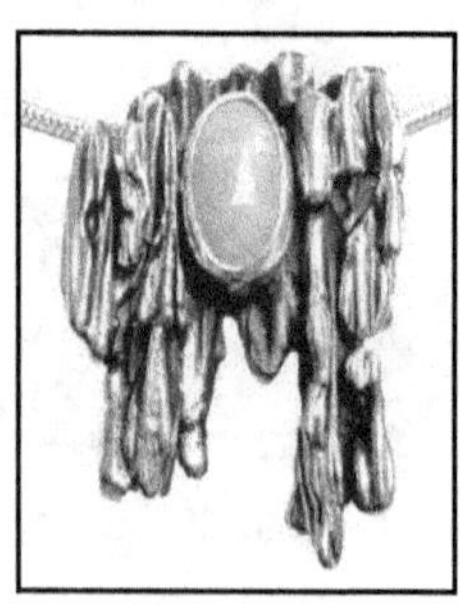

Bradford Smith

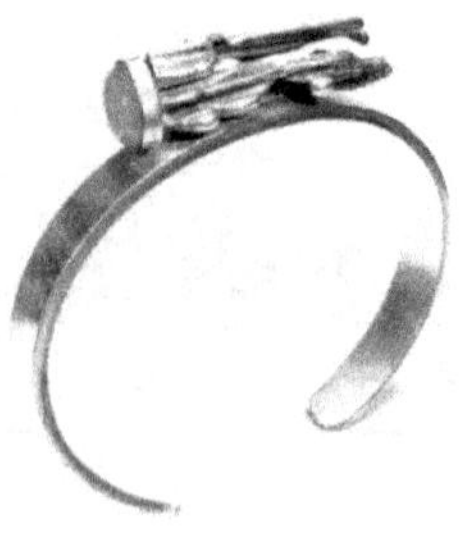

Eva Nathanson

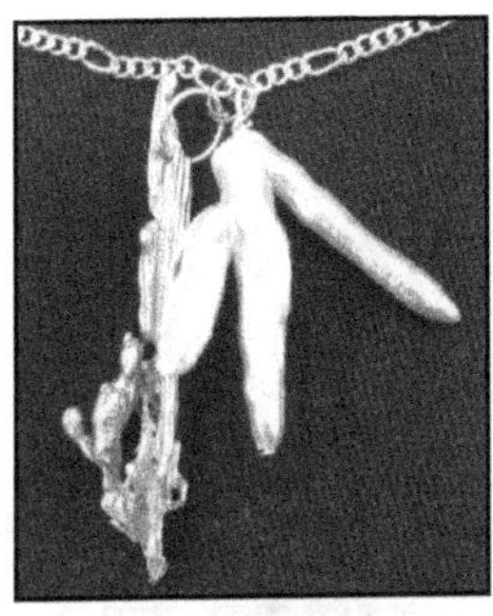

Sara Haium

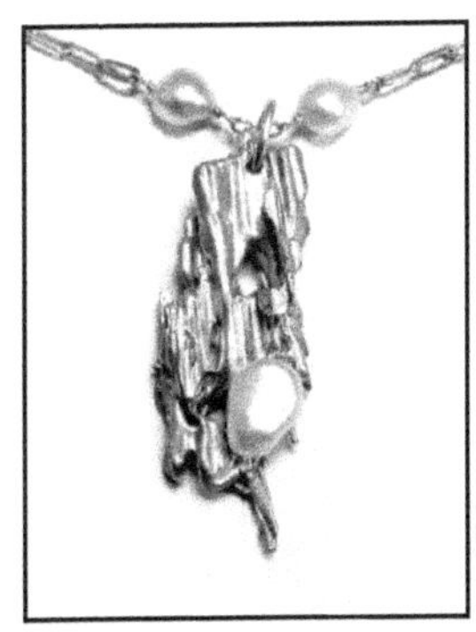

Hellena Jones Elbling

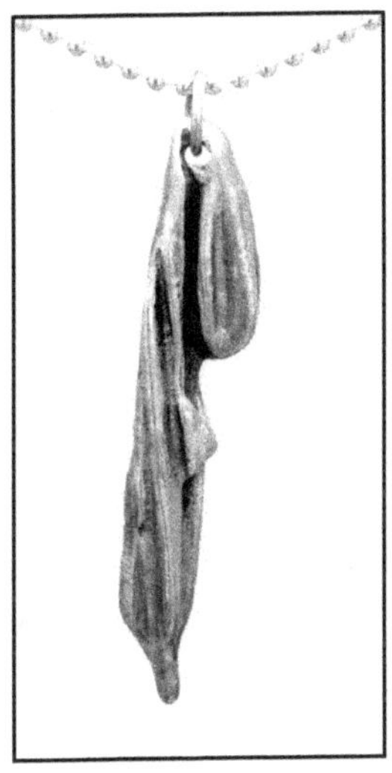

Bradford Smith

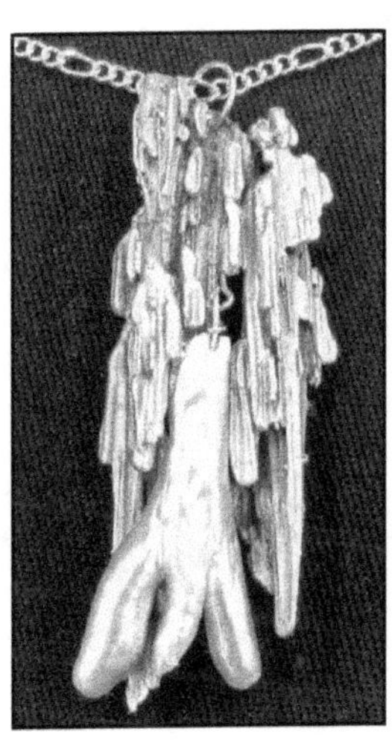

Sara Haium

A FAVOR PLEASE

Reviews are a significant way for books to gain visibility. As an independent author, I hope you enjoyed

Broom Casting for Creative Jewelry

and I'd truly appreciate it if you could post a few words of review on Amazon amazon.com/dp/0988285835

- Thank you

APPENDIX A

RUNNING A WORKSHOP

I have given demonstrations and taught many workshops on broom casting over the years. They have been a big hit with attendees, ages 18 to 87. And the workshops have been fun for me as well. If you are interested in doing one for your jewelry friends or for your rock and mineral club, here is everything that will be needed.

Outside of finding a convenient place to do the broom casting, one of the main difficulties in organizing a class or weekend workshop is figuring out what equipment will be needed. After forgetting a few important tools once or twice, I sat down and put together a good checklist that is given on the following page.

In addition, if anyone would like a copy of a sample workshop announcement or the handout material I give to attendees, email me at <BradSmithJewelry@yahoo.com>

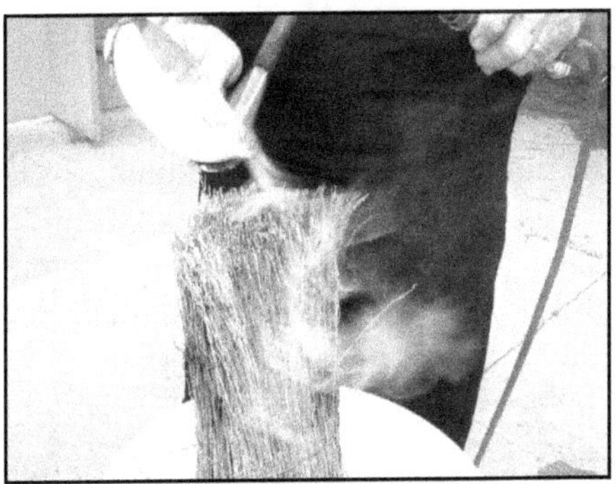

Workshop Supplies

This is a checklist of supplies that I have found useful to have on hand when doing a demonstration or teaching a broom casting workshop for up to eight people.

Tools & Supplies
===============

Torch
Large tip
Tank (full)
Chain to affix tank
Tank wrench
Lighter

Pickle pot
Extension cord
Pickle
Copper tongs
Four brooms
Binding wire
Four 5-gallon buckets
Shears to trim broom
Wire cutters
Round nose pliers
Sieve
Brass brushes
Steel brushes
Stylus picks

Fire extinguisher

Fireproof board
Fire bricks to make oven
Solder pads
2 x 4 blocks

Melting dish
Borax
Carbon stirring rod

2-3 oz Sterling for demos
Example castings & jewelry
Gram scale

Saw frames
Medium saw blades

Dremel motor tool
Small drills
Extension cord

PHOTO CREDITS

I would like to thank four of my students for allowing me to use pictures of their very creative broom cast designs.

Hellena Jones Elbling
Creations by Hellena
CreationsbyHellena@gmail.com
www.etsy.com/shop/CreationsbyHellena

Sara Haim
Sarandipity@earthlink.net

Eva P. Nathanson
Original Handcrafted Jewelry by Eva
www.etsy.com/shop/EvaNathansonJewelry
E.Nathanson@att.net

Ana Petrova
Los Angeles, CA
www.petrova.com

ABOUT THE AUTHOR

Brad Smith is a studio jeweler, lapidary, and jewelry instructor in Santa Monica, California. He is a long-time member of the Culver City Rock and Mineral Club, leading field trips, teaching lapidary skills, organizing gem & mineral shows, running workshops, and serving in club officer positions. He is also a member of the Metal Arts Society of Southern California.

His first book is the popular ***"Bench Tips for Jewelry Making"*** features 101 ways to solve common problems at the bench. It has received great reviews from the Florida Society of Goldsmiths and the Australian Facetors Guild, over thirty 5-star ratings on Amazon, and is frequently on Amazon's Top 100 Best Sellers List in the jewelry category.

Brad has been teaching Advanced Jewelry since 2002 in the Adult Education system of Los Angeles and Santa Monica, California. He writes a monthly column of jewelry making tips for over 200 newsletters in six countries.

In addition, he develops websites, as well as moderates jewelry making and rockhounding discussion groups online. He enjoys travel, photography, and scuba diving.

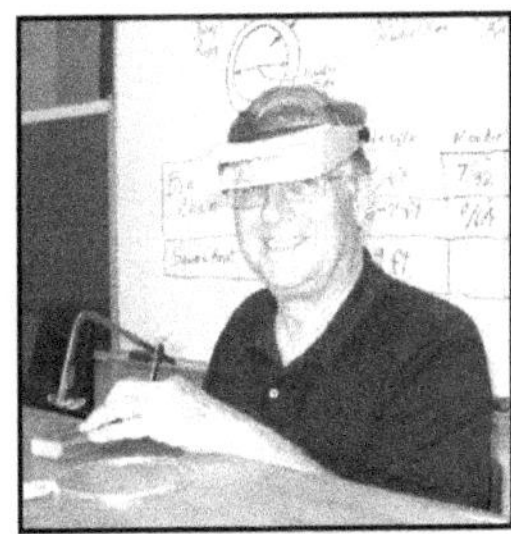

http://www.BradSmithJewelry.com

OTHER BOOKS BY THE AUTHOR

Making Design Stamps for Jewelry

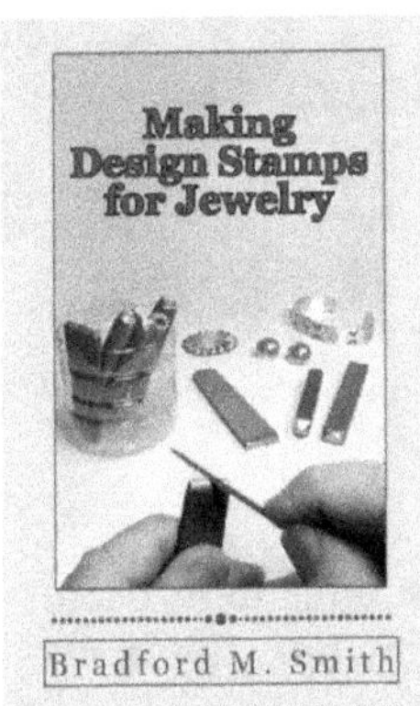

Learn how to create unique stamps and texturing tools to add visual interest to your work, for a special application, or to brand your pieces with a stamp that others cannot purchase. These custom tools embellish your jewelry designs and can be made with common jewelry tools and techniques. There are only a few differences in working with steel as compared to copper or silver.

The volume covers the step-by-step process of selecting best steels, carving the design, hardening the steel, and tempering it to ensure a long service life. It describes the tools to use, gives detailed examples for making several stamps, includes sources for tool steel, describes useful shop equipment, and has tips for saving time and achieving better quality.

amazon.com/dp/098828586X/

Editorial Review

"A must have book for the metalsmith"
- Danny Wade, Ferro Valley Tool, LLC and
creator of the Metal Stamp Addicts group on Facebook.

Amazon Reader Review

- This book is absolutely wonderful! If you are at all interested in the very least in making your own jewelry stamps, then you definitely need this book.

Accessories for the Foredom and Dremel

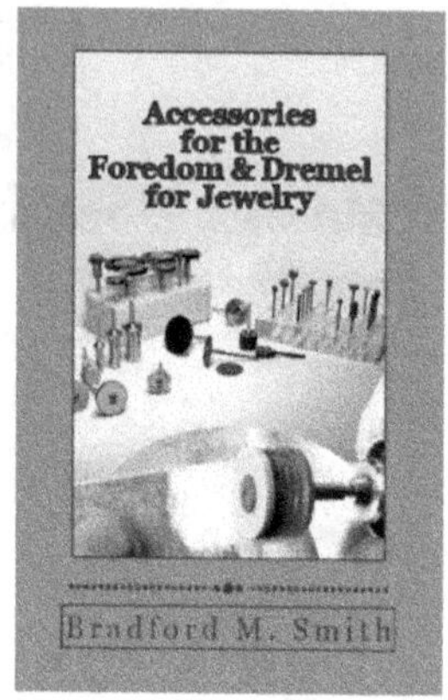

Flexible shaft and motor tools are an indispensable help to those who make jewelry, improving both the productivity and the quality of work. But with such an array of different tool bits to choose from, it's sometimes difficult to figure out the best one to use for each task.

"Accessories for the Foredom and Dremel" surveys the range of tool bits available for use with flexible shaft and hand-held motor tools and discusses the merits of each.

It highlights the best drill bits to use, the three most useful cutting burs, six different types of sanding bits, five ways to polish your work with the Foredom or Dremel, and five bits that can be used to add texture. In each category, I share my experience with the tool bits which save the most time, mention bench tips for getting the best results, and add cautions for safe use.

amazon.com/dp/0988285878/

Amazon Reader Reviews

- Five Stars - What a little treasure! … This book, while small, is packed full of great information on the subject. It's a great resource to keep handy at your bench.

- Five Stars - This is a wonderful book from someone that knows what he's talking about. Excellent tips and knowledge along the way.

- Five Stars - Love this book! Great reference book. Mr. Smith does a very good job of explaining how to choose the best tool bits for each job and how to use them to the best advantage.

Bench Tips for Jewelry Making

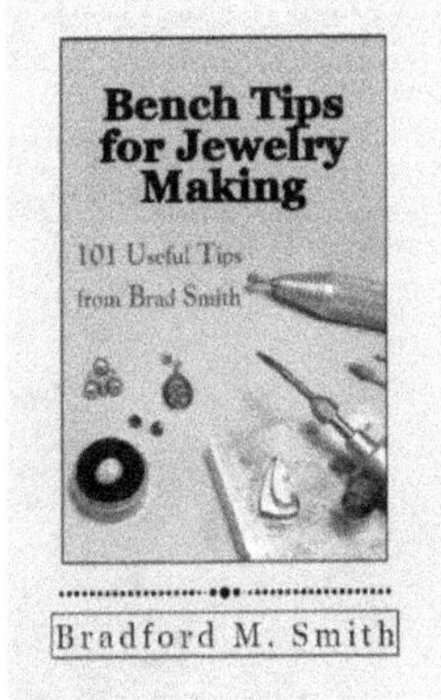

In every field, the top artisans have their favorite ways of solving common problems. Making a piece of fine jewelry is no exception. Accomplished jewelers have a variety of techniques, special tools and shortcuts that are proven to save time and improve quality.

This book is written as a resource for jewelers with skill levels from beginner to advanced. The bench tips come from Brad Smith's twenty years of experience in the jewelry industry, including over a decade teaching hundreds of students.

The tips include over twenty ways to save time when soldering and polishing, eight common hazards to avoid, many ways to cut costs, ten tips to improve stone setting skills, and the “must-have" tools for increasing productivity at the bench.

amazon.com/dp/0988285800/

Editorial Reviews

This small treasure covers a multitude of solutions to a myriad of issues facing the jewelry artisan…The easy to understand text and very good photographic black and white images makes this book quite self-explanatory…
- Razine Wenneker - Founder, The Society for Midwest Metalsmiths

This is a well written reference book by a very experienced studio jeweler and classroom instructor. The photographs and diagrams clearly point out the finer points of the various tips he demonstrates…
- Bruce Carlson - Florida Society of Goldsmiths Newsletter

More Bench Tips For Jewelry Making

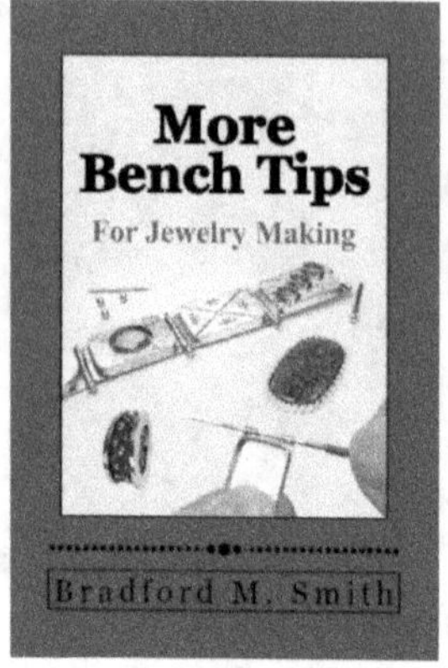

In every field top artisans have favorite ways of solving common problems. Making a piece of jewelry is no exception. Accomplished jewelers have shortcuts and special tools to help them save time and increase the quality of the work.

This second volume of Bench Tips includes 86 ways to save time, avoid frustration or improve quality in areas of fabrication, stone setting, casting, soldering and polishing.

These tips from the author's extensive shop experience will help you get the most out of your tools, keep costs under control, and avoid common hazards. "More Bench Tips" is written as a resource for jewelers with skill levels from beginner through advanced.

amazon.com/dp/ 0988285886/

Amazon Reader Reviews

- Easy to understand writing style, clear and concise instructions. Absolute MUST have for any artisan --beginner and advanced alike.

- This is my third book from this author. Very informative and nice techniques are mentioned in this book. What I like is these information does not overlap with my other books. I got much more than what I paid for this book! No doubt 5 stars.

- I own and treasure the first book, Bench Tips. This is a great sequel to that book. Very good tips and useful information for the beginner and advanced metal smith.

The Reluctant Farmer of Whimsey Hill

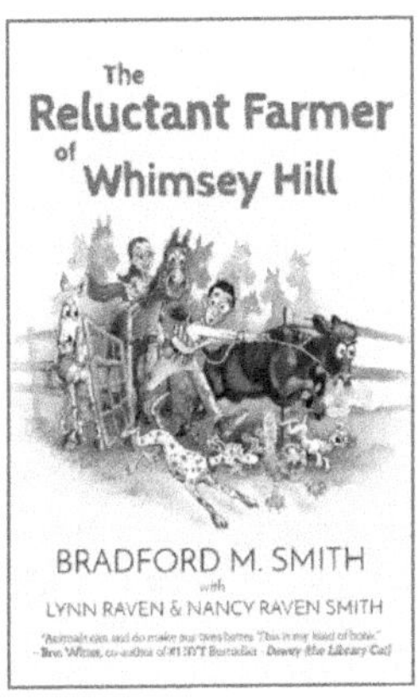

The Reluctant Farmer of Whimsey Hill is a light-hearted, true love story between more than a man and a woman. Imagine *Marley and Me*, not with one pesky dog, but with a farm full of quirky animals. The narrative follows Brad's fish-out-of-water point of view as a 25-year-old, animal-phobic, computer nerd from the city who moves to a rural, Virginia farm with his new, animal-loving bride. There he's propelled on a journey of self-discovery as his bride's crazy animals teach him about life - the hard way.

amazon.com/dp/0988285851/

Editorial Reviews

- Animals can and do make our lives better. This is my kind of book.
- Bret Witter, #1 NYT bestseller and co-author of Dewey [the Library Cat]

- A witty memoir reminding us that the best lessons in life are beyond the edge of one's comfort zone, and one can only be towed there by the heart strings."
- Jean Abernethy, creator of Fergus the Horse

Amazon Reader Reviews

- Anyone who loves animals, has a sense of humor and appreciates a good, clean book (plenty of mud though) will love this book!

- A charming, witty, well written account of the country life of a young couple, with some sweet moments and some laugh out loud moments. We thoroughly enjoyed it.

www.ingramcontent.com/pod-product-compliance
Lightning Source LLC
LaVergne TN
LVHW010945110826
845149LV00013B/2761
* 9 7 8 0 9 8 8 2 8 5 8 3 5 *